WOULD YOU OR RATHER?

Book For Kids 6-12 Years Old

200 Funny Scenarios, Wacky Choices and Hilarious Situations for the Whole Family

With Fun Illustrations

Riddleland

TABLE OF CONTENTS

INTRODUCTION

"The important thing is not to stop questioning"

~ Albert Einstein

We would like to personally thank you for purchasing this book. The **Would You Rather Book for Kids 6-12 years old** is a collection of 200 of the funniest scenarios, wacky choices, and hilarious situations for kids to choose from. It is also filled with fun and cute illustrations.

These questions are an excellent way to get a conversation started in a fun and exciting way. Also, by asking "Why?" after a "Would you rather" question, you may find interesting answers and learn a lot about a person.

We wrote this book because we want children to be encouraged to read more, think, and grow. As parents, we know that when children play games and learn, they are being educated while having so much fun that they don't even realize they're learning and developing valuable life skills. 'Would you Rather ...' is one of our favorite games to play as a family. Some of the 'would you rather ...' scenarios have had us in fits of giggles, others have generated reactions such as: "Eeeeeeuuugh, that's gross!" and yet others still really make us think and reflect and consider our decisions.

Besides having fun, playing the game also has other benefits such as:

> **Communication** – This game helps children to interact, read aloud, and listen to others. It's a great way to connect. It's a fun way for parents to get their children interacting with them without a formal, awkward conversation. The game can also help to get to know someone better and learn about their likes, dislikes, and values.

> **Builds Confidence** - Children get used to pronouncing vocabulary, asking questions and it helps to deal with shyness.

> **Develops Critical Thinking** – It helps children to defend and justify the rationale for their choices and can generate discussions and debates. Parents playing this game with young children can give them prompting questions about their answers to help them reach logical and sensible decisions.

> **Improves Vocabulary** – Children will be introduced to new words in the questions, and the context of them will help them remember them because the game is fun.

> **Encourages Equality and Diversity** – Considering other people's answers, even if they differ from your own, is important for respect, equality, diversity, tolerance, acceptance, and inclusivity. Some questions may get children to think about options available to them, that don't fall into gendered stereotypes, i.e., careers or activities that challenge the norm.

RULES OF THE GAME

This game is probably best played with other people, so if you can, play it with friends or family

If you have two players

> > > > > > > > > >

> Player 1 takes the book and asks the player 2 a question beginning with the phrase, "Would you rather...? Why?"

> After player 2 makes his/her choice, he/she has to explain the reason why the choice was made.

> Pass the book to the other player, and they ask you a question.

> Learn lots about one another, have fun and giggles.

> The Two-Player game version could work well as an ice-breaker exercise before introductions in classes or meetings.

If you have three or four players

> > > > > > > > > > >

> Out of your group, decide who will be the Question Master. If you can't decide, have folded bits of paper with 'Question Master' written on one, and 'players' on the other and each pick one.

> The Question Master asks one question from the book.

> The other two or three people give their answers.

> The Question Master decides who has given the best answer – this is the answer with the best explanation for why. The explanations can be funny or creative or well thought out. The Question Master's decision is final. One point is given for the best answer. If the Question Master can't decide, both players get one point each.

> The first player to reach a score of 10 points wins.

Let The Fun Begin

7

Riddleland Bonus

Join our **Facebook Group** at **Riddleland for Kids**
to get daily jokes and riddles.

> > > > > > > > > > > > > > > > > > > >

https://pixelfy.me/riddlelandbonus

Thank you for buying this book. As a token of our appreciation,
we would like to offer a special bonus—a collection of
50 original jokes, riddles, and funny stories.

For the rest of your life: eat everything with a fork that has only one prong

OR

eat everything with a spoon that was chewed up by a waste disposal?

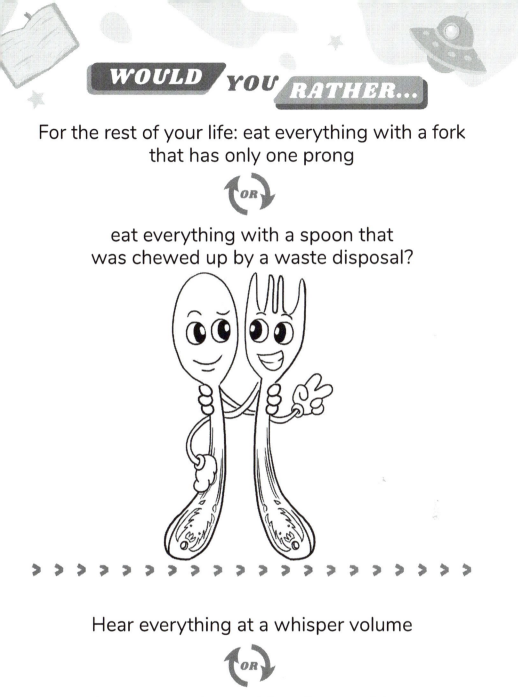

Hear everything at a whisper volume

OR

lose your voice and "say" everything through body language?

Drink a big green leafy spinach smoothie

crunch into a fresh, tart lemon each
morning for breakfast?

> > > > > > > > > > > > > > > > > > >

Eat frozen peas for dinner every day
all winter long

OR

slurp a hot bowl of chili for dinner
every day throughout the summer?

Eat a whole cake's worth of buttercream icing

OR

a whole tub of plain vanilla ice-cream for dinner every night for one month?

Have a clone who goes to school and does all of your chores

OR

have the ability to mind control other people's thoughts?

Find a treasure box full of half-melted chocolate bars

a bunch of old and hard Gummy Bears?

Touch a person, and this makes them incapable of lying

touch a person and heal whatever is wrong with them?

Be a cool wizard with no powers

OR

an ugly goblin with awesome powers?

Snap your fingers, and your lost
items appear

OR

snap your fingers to get your bedroom
to tidy itself?

Slide down a water slide like a fish

climb a treehouse playset like a monkey?

> > > > > > > > > > > > > > > > > > > >

Discover the underwater lost city
of Atlantis

discover alien life at Area 51?

Ride standing up on a camel's hump

ride sitting down on an elephant's trunk?

Try to eat ice-cream being thrown at your face

try to drink a milkshake that is dripping off the top of your head?

Be able to fly for an hour each Friday

OR

be super strong from 7-9am on Mondays?

Make food appear when you think of it

OR

travel anywhere in the world by just
looking at a picture?

Visit the past and turn into a dinosaur

turn into a caveman before fire was discovered?

> >

Have the ability to travel into the
future and take only one photograph

spend an hour in the past with someone who is no
longer living (family
or famous)?

Be a horse tamer, always riding
wild and crazy horses

be an artist with paint on your face all the time?

> > > > > > > > > > > > > > > > > > > >

Only see blue when the sun shines

only see grey when the moon is out?

WOULD YOU RATHER...

Step on the tail of a squeaky mouse

OR

eat two dirt covered worms?

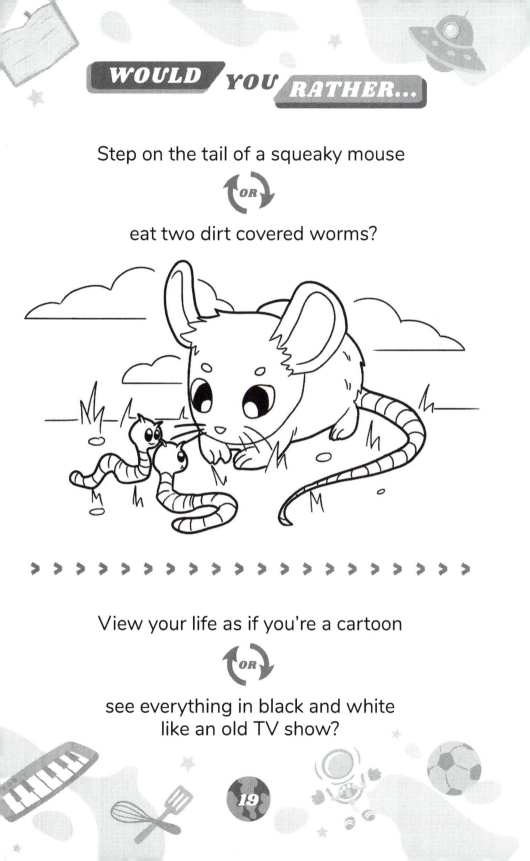

> > > > > > > > > > > > > > > > > > > >

View your life as if you're a cartoon

OR

see everything in black and white
like an old TV show?

WOULD YOU RATHER...

Be a child who's always getting in trouble

a rule following grownup your whole life?

> > > > > > > > > > > > > > > > > > >

Go to detention every day for
a whole year

Get homework every day for one year?

Be trapped in a cage full of hissing snakes

a cage full of chomping crocodiles?

Eat five hot chili peppers with
nothing to drink

drink a chili-flavoured milkshake?

Step on a worm and start to cry

step on an anthill and start to itch?

Spend your best friend's pocket-money
on yourself

spend your pocket-money on your
best friend?

Have a genie grant three wishes
all at once

OR

get one wish every five years?

Be able to eat whatever you want
whenever you want

OR

go to bed whenever you want only
if you want to?

WOULD YOU RATHER...

Remain young like a child until your 70th birthday

OR

get an instant career like you're 35 years old now?

Grow yummy vegetables by spitting on the ground

OR

make it rain whenever you clap your hands?

Understand the secret chirping language of birds

OR

the purring and hissing of cats?

Never bathe or shower but always smell good

OR

never have to cut your hair again because it always looks the same?

Have a long beard that houses wildlife

a very hairy body like the yeti?

> > > > > > > > > > > > > > > > > > > >

Be able to speed-read books and
always remember them

be able to re-watch any movie you've
ever seen just by thinking about
it in your head?

Be able to draw things that come to life

write stories that become true?

Never have a scary nightmare again

always dream about fluffy pink unicorns
leaping over rainbow clouds?

WOULD YOU RATHER...

Be able to see colours without using your eyes

make music with your nose?

> > > > > > > > > > > > > > > > > > > >

Be able to hold your breath for as long as you want

be able to stop blinking and win any staring contest?

Have a bear that has been declawed

OR

have a lion that has no teeth for a pet?

Have a dozen eggs cracked on top of
your head

OR

a bottle of tomato-ketchup explode
all over your shirt?

Drink of a cup of thick, brown mud

OR

a cup of hot chocolate spiced with red pepper?

> >

Go back in time to meet up with loved ones who have passed away

OR

go to the future to meet up with your children or grandchildren?

Have a billion pounds that you can spend on anything you want for yourself only

OR

have a big bag full of £100 notes to give to anyone you see in need?

Build your house on a playground

OR

live at a zoo full of animals?

Eat a birthday cake made from spinach

OR

a cupcake iced with slimy onions?

Be stuck outside naked in a snowstorm

OR

be outside wearing a snowsuit during a thunderstorm?

WOULD YOU RATHER...

Get stung by a bee every month

OR

bit by an angry mosquito every day for a year?

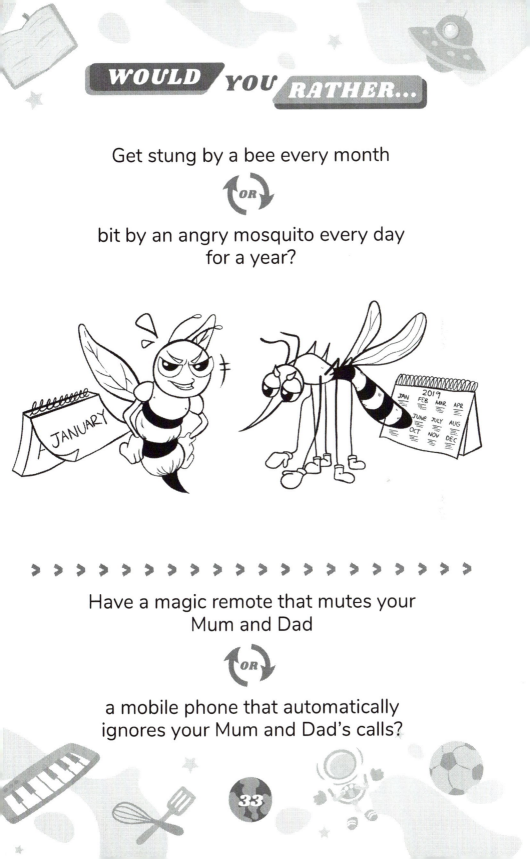

Have a magic remote that mutes your Mum and Dad

OR

a mobile phone that automatically ignores your Mum and Dad's calls?

WOULD YOU RATHER...

Be able to play any musical instrument

be able to nail any dance moves that you try?

> > > > > > > > > > > > > > > > > > > >

Change one thing about yourself

change one thing about your Mum or Dad?

WOULD YOU RATHER...

Give your best friend a gift that you didn't want

give your parents a homemade present?

> > > > > > > > > > > > > > > > > > > >

Go to work one day for either your Mum or Dad, and have them go to school for you

spend one day with your parents when they were the same age as you and you can hang out together?

35

Have to buy a new pair of shoes each week because yours get too stinky

OR

have to buy new clothes every week because they get holes in them?

>>>>>>>>>>>>>>>>>>>>>>

Tell your Mum what to do for a day

OR

tell your Dad what to do for a day?

Have Wonder Woman's super strength

Batgirl's super gadgets?

Live in a decked-out camping tent with multiple rooms and electricity

have a wall-sized TV in your room hooked up to every game console?

Be a super-nerdy Science Teacher

or

a Doctor who is super shy?

Know how to code in 5 different programming languages

or

be able to speak Russian, English, Mandarin, Japanese, and Arabic?

Get an A+ grade on every school exam

win every sports game at school?

Fly around the world without getting jetlag

be able to run a marathon without being tired?

Go to school wearing a red clown's nose

OR

go to school wearing a big blue curly clown's wig?

Have the floors of your house bouncy like a trampoline

OR

the walls bouncy like a giant blow-up bouncy house?

Have a giant but friendly
house-sized mouse

OR

a tiny but fierce pet elephant?

Eat an apple that has worms inside of it

OR

eat a bowl of fresh tinned dog food?

Kiss a big green hopping frog

cuddle a hairy black tarantula?

Have to clean your room every day
but only get homework once a week

get homework every day but only have
to clean your room once a week?

Own a friendly fire-breathing dragon

own a grumpy rainbow-maned unicorn?

Go to the dentist to get a hole in your tooth filled

go to the doctor for a vaccination injection?

Have a pet lion who snuggles with you

OR

have a pet tiger who jumps through hoops of fire?

> >

Breathe underwater like a fish

OR

run across the top of oceans, seas, and lakes?

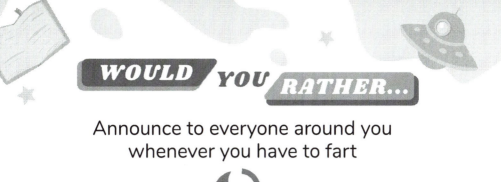

Announce to everyone around you
whenever you have to fart

announce when you have to poop?

> > > > > > > > > > > > > > > > > > > >

Be able to make things teeny tiny

blow things up to a jumbo size
using only the power of your mind?

45

Have a pet fish who can talk

a fish that can take walks on a lead?

> > > > > > > > > > > > > > > > > > > >

Be a superhero, but you can never
reveal your identity

be a supervillain, and everyone knows
who you are?

Turn into a unicorn that can grant wishes

or a mermaid who can control the sea?

> > > > > > > > > > > > > > > > > > >

Be able to bend things with your mind

be able to lift things with your mind?

WOULD YOU RATHER...

Start every sentence with, "Hey smelly."

end every sentence with "... oopsy daisy"?

> > > > > > > > > > > > > > > > > > > >

Have the power to camouflage yourself
like a chameleon

have the ability to turn into
anything or anyone?

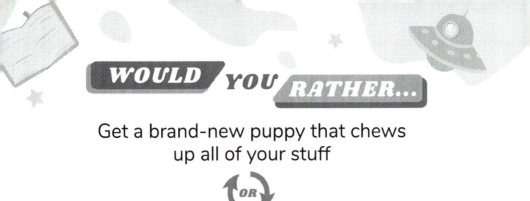

Get a brand-new puppy that chews
up all of your stuff

OR

be able to buy a new toy every month?

Be able to turn invisible

OR

change into a monster when you're angry?

Never eat yummy delicious sweets again

OR

never drink sweet sugary pop again for the rest of your life?

> > > > > > > > > > > > > > > > > > > >

Live near mountains known to be home to an abominable snowman

OR

near a lake known to be home to a sea monster?

Eat garlic flavoured ice cream with crunchy pieces of garlic

OR

bite into an onion flavoured marshmallow?

> > > > > > > > > > > > > > > > > > >

Have your friends secretly read your diary behind your back

OR

do the chicken dance by yourself every time you hang out with your friends?

Have the sharp eyes of an eagle

the sharp teeth of a beaver?

Laugh out loud whenever someone farts

be laughed at every time that you fart, no matter how silent?

Hop long distances like a kangaroo

or

zig-zag at high speed like a crab?

Go to bed one hour earlier than you need to

or

take a cold shower every morning?

Live in a muddy sty with a greedy pig

OR

in a warm, smelly and loud chicken coop?

> >

Be the smartest human alive

OR

be able to turn into any animal?

Never be able to eat waffles again

or

never be able to eat pancakes with syrup again?

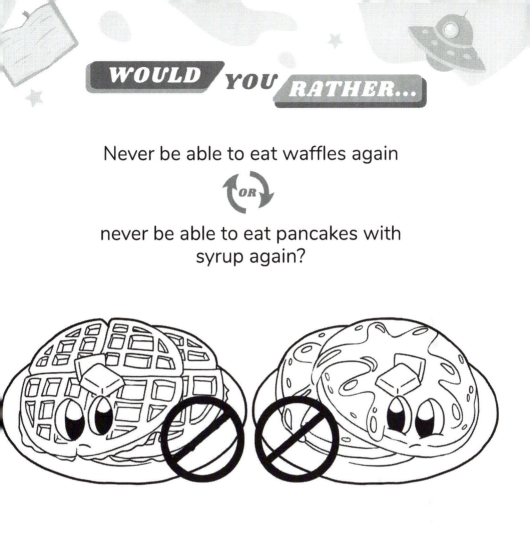

Have to hunt for every piece of meat

or

have to grow every vegetable that you eat from now on?

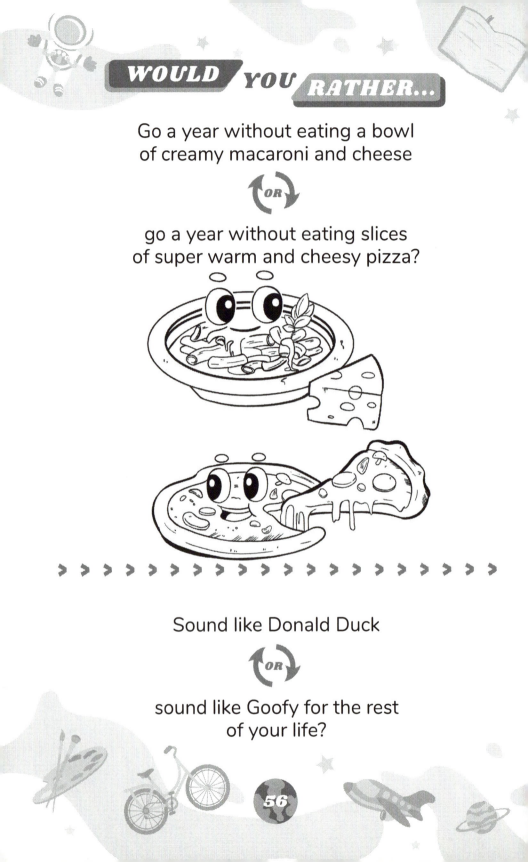

Go a year without eating a bowl of creamy macaroni and cheese

OR

go a year without eating slices of super warm and cheesy pizza?

Sound like Donald Duck

OR

sound like Goofy for the rest of your life?

Eat big raw bunches of leafy green broccoli

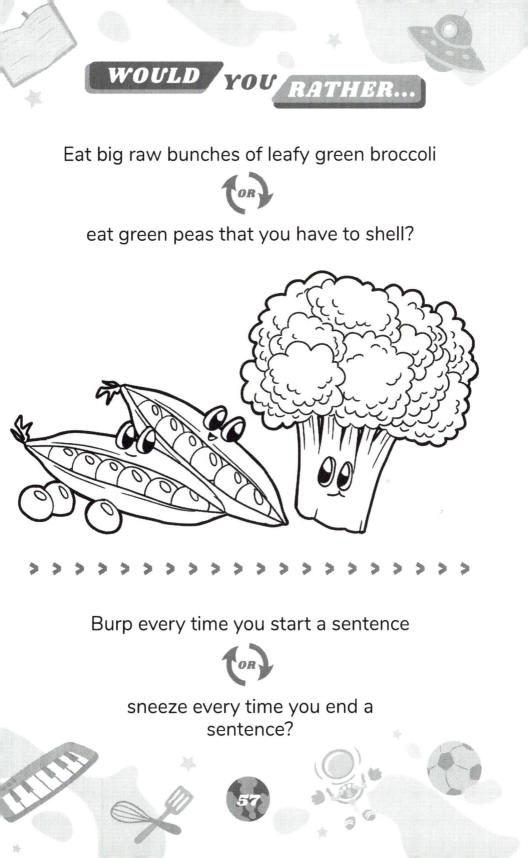

eat green peas that you have to shell?

> >

Burp every time you start a sentence

OR

sneeze every time you end a sentence?

It rained all flavours of jellybeans

OR

snowed sticky sugary pink candyfloss?

> > > > > > > > > > > > > > > > > > > >

Have toilet water poured on your head

OR

a rotten egg cracked on your head?

WOULD YOU RATHER...

Eat every meal standing up

OR

drink every liquid laying down?

>>>>>>>>>>>>>>>>>>>>>

Be a famous singer who gets laryngitis

OR

a famous actor/actress who has stage fright?

Spend a whole day in the cold ocean swimming with dolphins

OR

a whole day in the hot jungle climbing trees with monkeys?

> > > > > > > > > > > > > > > > > > > >

Be very famous for something silly

OR

be very talented and no one knows your name?

WOULD YOU RATHER...

Eat a bowl of saucy spaghetti with only your hands

eat an entire bowl of soup with a fork?

> > > > > > > > > > > > > > > > > > > >

Not be able to taste anything sweet

OR

only be able to taste sour things?

Have a cat who is bigger than
a hippopotamus

OR

a hippopotamus the size of your
house cat?

Spend an hour with ten kittens crawling
all over you

OR

spend an hour with ten puppies licking
all over your face?

Live in a flying hot air balloon for a week

OR

live submerged in a submarine for a week?

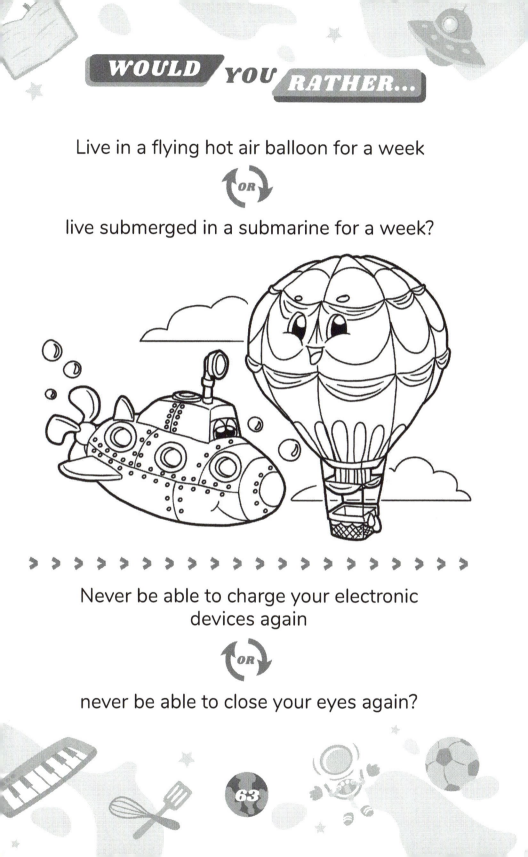

> > > > > > > > > > > > > > > > > > > >

Never be able to charge your electronic devices again

OR

never be able to close your eyes again?

WOULD YOU RATHER...

Grow sharp-clawed tiger paws
on your hands

OR

grow a big, long elephant's trunk
from your face?

> >

Skip school to watch TV at home for
one entire day

OR

spend one day at school watching TV
with your classmates?

Turn completely red and live on Mars

OR

grow rings around your body and live on Jupiter?

Go to school for eight hours every night

OR

have forks and spoons instead of fingers?

Turn into the big green Incredible Hulk when you are angry

OR

turn into super strong Thor with his magic hammer?

> > > > > > > > > > > > > > > > > >

Have your favourite teacher eat dinner with your family

OR

go to your favourite teacher's house and eat dinner with his or her family?

Turn into an eagle and soar in the sky looking for mice and rats to snatch up

OR

turn into a giant blue whale and swallow literally tons of krill each day?

Be a super sneaky stealthy ninja

OR

a strong graceful ballet dancer?

Be covered in thick white fur like
a polar bear

have the smooth bare skin
of a Siamese cat?

> > > > > > > > > > > > > > > > > > > >

Have a sliding trombone instead of a nose

OR

a loud megaphone instead of a mouth?

Be an astronaut traveling to another planet in a rocket

OR

an alien visiting Earth in a spaceship?

> > > > > > > > > > > > > > > > > > > >

Have a dog that purrs & hisses like a cat

OR

a cat that barks and wags its tail like a dog?

Eat one plain piece of bread

a plain bowl of rice every day for lunch?

Step on a giant sticky wad of chewing-gum

a pile of super slippery round chewing-gum balls?

Be an astronaut in space who runs out of oxygen

OR

a deep-sea diver deep in the ocean who runs out of oxygen?

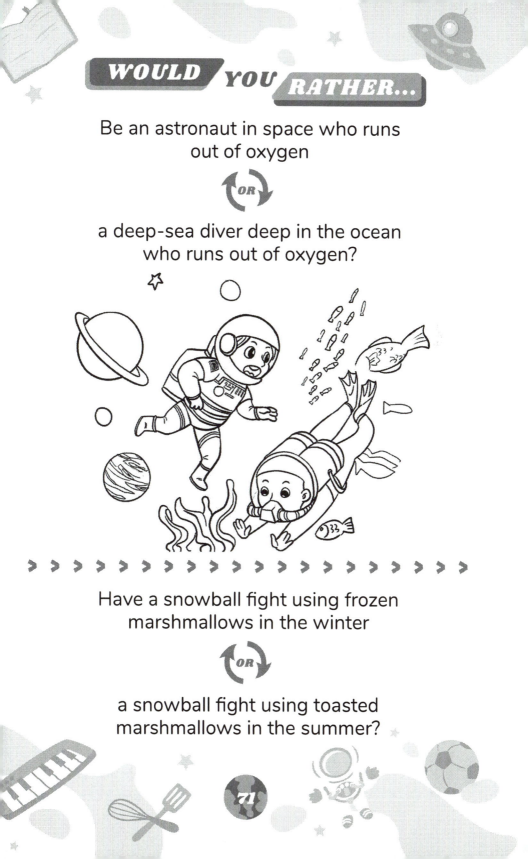

Have a snowball fight using frozen marshmallows in the winter

OR

a snowball fight using toasted marshmallows in the summer?

Be a minotaur with a half-human, half-bull body

OR

a centaur with a half-human, half-horse body?

Have a photographic memory and never forget a thing

OR

have a nose that never forgets a smell?

Be the King of the Jungle – the Majestic Lion King

OR

King of the Sea – The Ferocious Great White Shark?

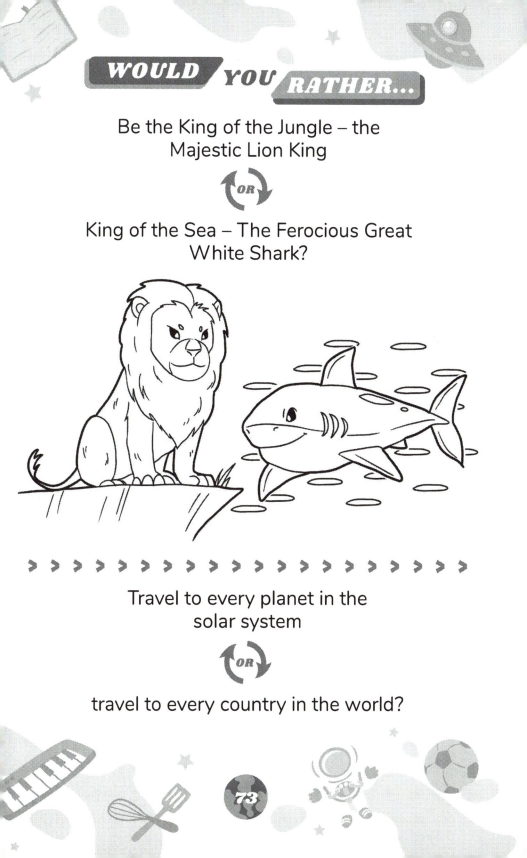

Travel to every planet in the solar system

OR

travel to every country in the world?

Eat a big green watermelon that tastes like a super sweet cantaloupe

eat a big orange cantaloupe that tastes juicy and seedy like a strawberry?

> > > > > > > > > > > > > > > > > > > >

Tell your friends that you sing opera

tell your friends that you love to country line dance?

Eat a bacon caramel cottage
cheese sundae

OR

a tofu cheese cupcake with
Gummy Bears?

Mow the lawn on the hottest day
of summer

OR

shovel snow on the coldest day
of winter?

Be a tornado hunter tracking
an F5 tornado

be running away from a fast moving
and powerful hurricane?

> > > > > > > > > > > > > > > > > > >

Have the power to see anything
in the world

the power to hear any sound
in the world?

Walk one mile through deep
and heavy snow

OR

walk one mile through a downpour of rain?

> > > > > > > > > > > > > > > > > > > >

Get to wherever you're going by doing cartwheels
the whole way

OR

by rolling dizzying somersaults?

Have a laugh that sounds like a kitten meowing

a laugh that sounds like a dog barking?

Live in a very grand old castle with lots of musty rooms

live in a really small grass hut with a beautiful beach and ocean view?

WOULD YOU RATHER...

Get one big and super awesome present
for Christmas every 10 years

OR

ten small and okay presents for
Christmas every year?

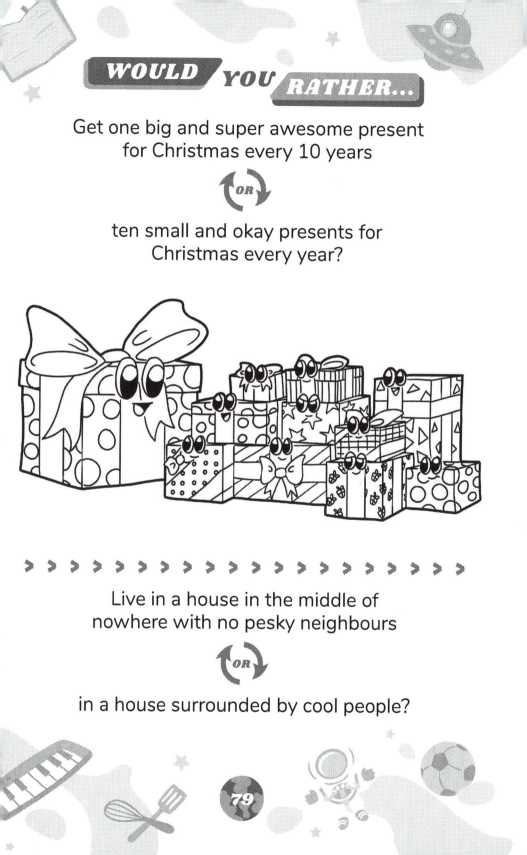

> > > > > > > > > > > > > > > > > > > >

Live in a house in the middle of
nowhere with no pesky neighbours

OR

in a house surrounded by cool people?

Live on a spaceship with all sorts of high-tech alien gadgets

OR

live on an island filled with every kind of dessert imaginable?

> >

Have a super annoying habit you can't quit

OR

a really awful smell coming from some part of your body?

WOULD YOU RATHER...

Wake up before the sun rises
every morning

OR

go to bed before the sun sets
every night?

Be a king or queen with no friends

OR

live in a house where no one has their
own room, but you all get along?

Live on a boat and never step on land

OR

live on an island and never be able
to leave?

Stay up all night helping a family
member fix their problem

OR

spend all of your screen time
doing chores?

Get locked out of your phone for one day

OR

get a giant crack in your screen that keeps getting bigger?

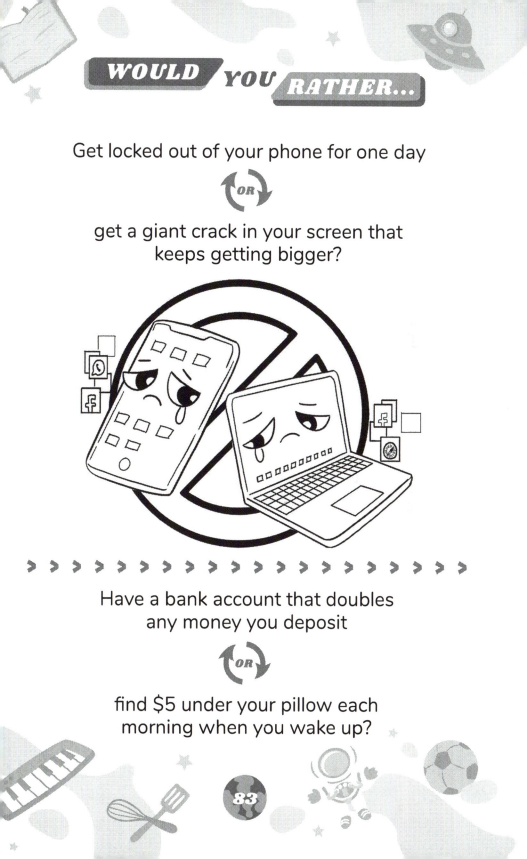

Have a bank account that doubles any money you deposit

OR

find $5 under your pillow each morning when you wake up?

Give up all of your screen time
for one whole year

OR

give up listening to any kind of music
for one whole year?

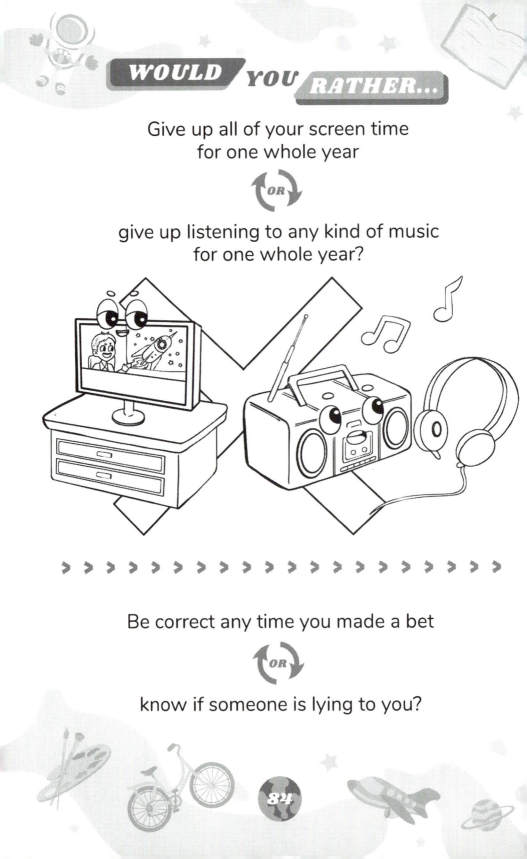

Be correct any time you made a bet

OR

know if someone is lying to you?

Be an amazing artist who is tone deaf (can't hear musical tones)

OR

a piano player who can't even draw a stick man?

Have only your right or left hand

OR

have three really tiny hands?

Go sky diving from 3000 meters

or

go bungee jumping from 300 meters
on a windy day?

Have a lifetime's supply of your
favourite chocolate bar

or

have a famous chocolate bar named
after you?

Be able to play the guitar but have to clip your nails every day

OR

be able to play the violin and have to use your own hair to make the bow?

Eat a dirt-flavoured ice cream cone

OR

eat an earwax flavoured peach crumble?

Be the fire-breathing dragon

OR

the rise-from-the-ashes phoenix in a battle between the two creatures?

> > > > > > > > > > > > > > > > > > > >

Have a hundred good friends

OR

ten best friends?

Live in a castle with stone cold floors
and walls

OR

in a wooden cabin with a dirt floor
and dusty interior?

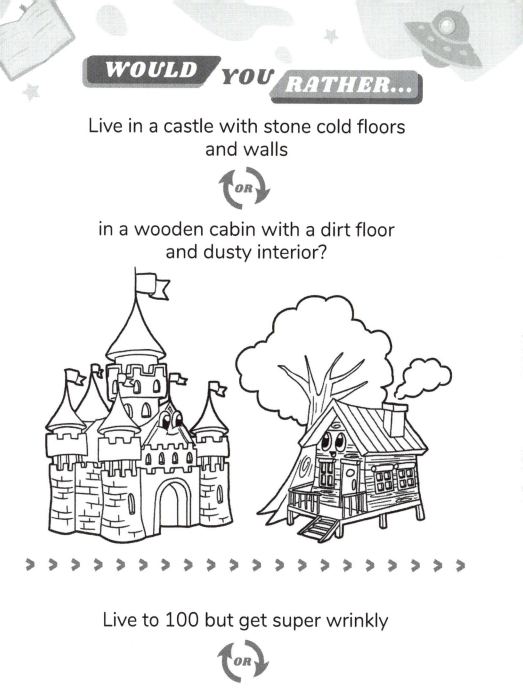

Live to 100 but get super wrinkly

OR

turn into a metal robot and live forever?

Eat a lime like an apple

suck all of the juice from a lemon?

> > > > > > > > > > > > > > > > > > > >

Be a superhero and fight crime

be a super villain and commit all kinds
of crimes?

Have a top-secret hideout treehouse

OR

a super bouncy trampoline
in your backyard?

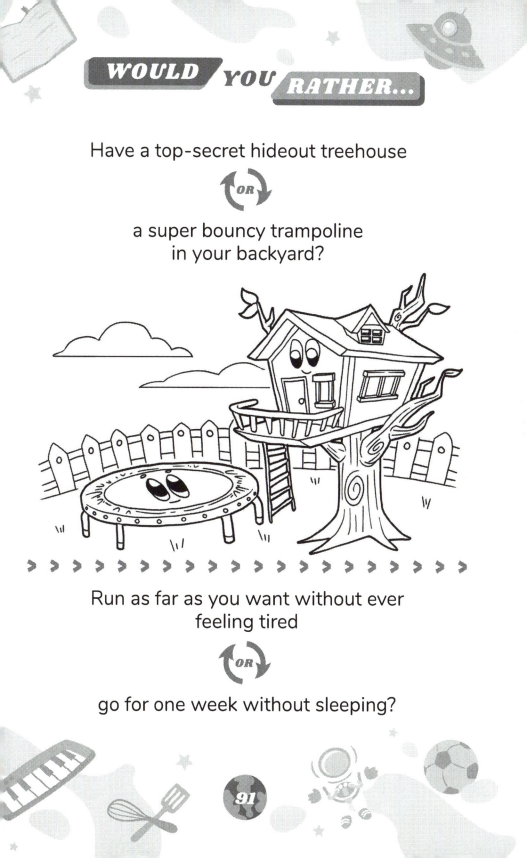

Run as far as you want without ever
feeling tired

OR

go for one week without sleeping?

Stumble across a moose in the forest

be chased by a mountain goat down the side of a mountain?

Visit an aquarium and dive in

OR

visit a zoo and climb into the llama enclosure?

Eat baby back ribs with syrup
every morning

OR

eat a stack of pancakes with BBQ
sauce every night

Never play a video game again

OR

never get so much as a sniffle again?

Have painted on stripes like a zebra

have the really long neck of a giraffe?

Downhill ski with only one pole

water ski with only one ski?

WOULD YOU RATHER...

Wash your hair once a month

OR

brush your teeth once a month?

Make an important speech

OR

perform a dance in front
of a thousand people?

Eat dry cereal with no milk every meal
for a week

OR

eat frozen waffles every meal
for a week?

> > > > > > > > > > > > > > > > > > >

Be able to predict the future and unable
to change it

OR

be able to change the future but not
see what will happen?

Learn how to fish using only your hands

learn how to hunt using only your hands?

Get amnesia and forget who you are

have memory loss and forget everything else in your life?

Take one month to learn how to juggle five balls

OR

take one week and lots of falls to learn how to ride a unicycle?

> >

See everything upside down

OR

hear everything backward?

Be able to walk through any wall

OR

be able to turn invisible on demand?

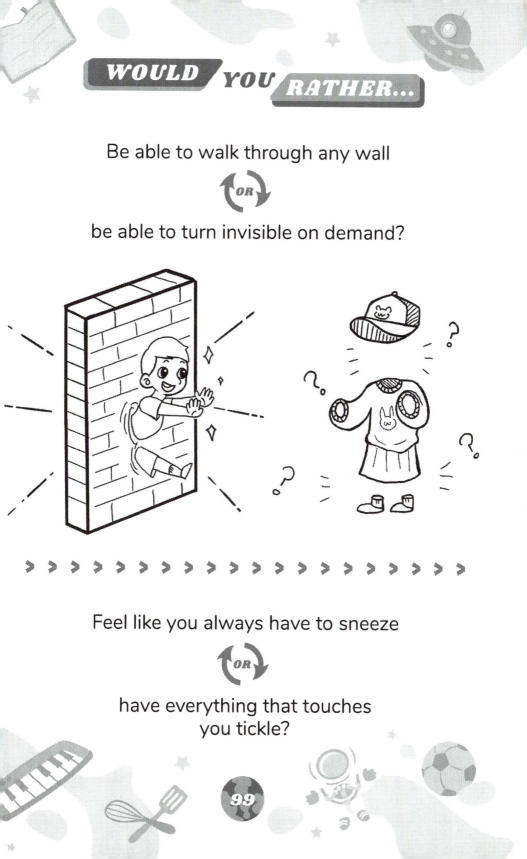

Feel like you always have to sneeze

OR

have everything that touches you tickle?

WOULD YOU RATHER...

Eat smelly brown rotten vegetables

eat fuzzy green mouldy bread?

Work a job making £10 per hour that
you can spend on yourself

be an unpaid volunteer for a charity
that really helps people?

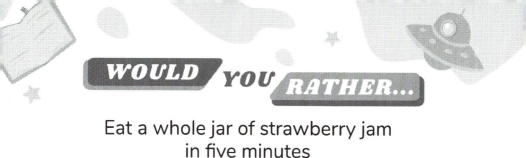
Eat a whole jar of strawberry jam
in five minutes

drink a cup of hot sauce in one hour?

> > > > > > > > > > > > > > > > > > >

Have suction cups at the end of each finger

have bells at the end of each toe?

Jump into a pool of thick rich dark chocolate pudding

OR

jump into a pool of chunky fruity blueberry ice cream?

> > > > > > > > > > > > > > > > > > >

Lose the ability to speak and hear

OR

lose the ability to see things?

Eat a can of cat food after your cat licked out of it

OR

eat a piece of raw fish that your cat chewed on?

Always laugh when you want to cry

OR

always cry when you want to laugh?

Have a low-pitched voice like a gorilla

a high-pitched voice like a baby?

Go to school two days a week every
week of the year

go to school seven days a week for six
months of the year?

Brush your teeth with hot sauce flavoured toothpaste

OR

brush your teeth with mayonnaise straight from the jar?

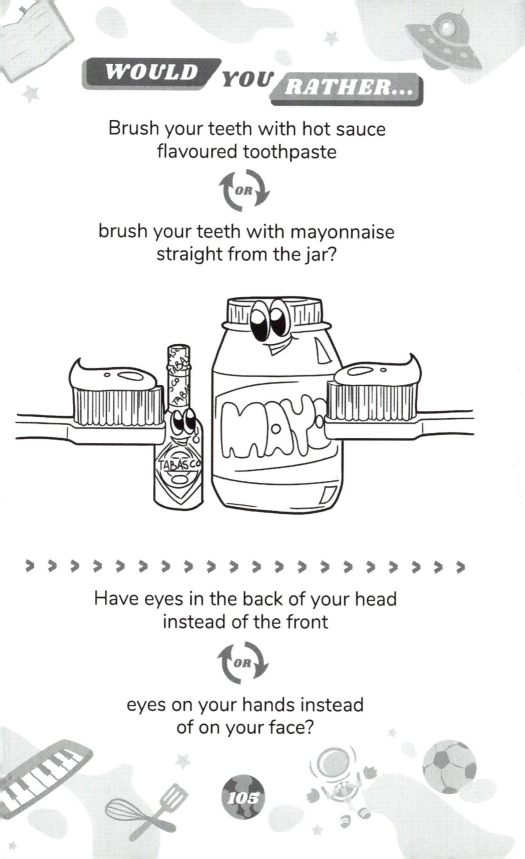

Have eyes in the back of your head instead of the front

OR

eyes on your hands instead of on your face?

Wear clothes completely covered with polka dots

wear checkered clothes that look like a noughts and crosses board?

> > > > > > > > > > > > > > > > > > > >

Play one game of chess for six hours

connect 50,000 numbers in a dot-to-dot?

Be a cobra snake with no poison

OR

be a scorpion with a broken stinger?

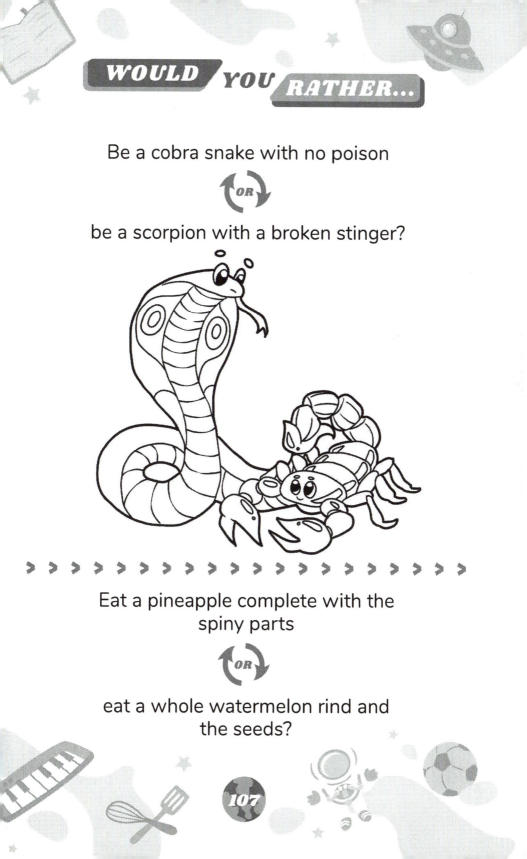

Eat a pineapple complete with the spiny parts

OR

eat a whole watermelon rind and the seeds?

Be a winged fairy that can't fly

OR

be a toy elf that can only make broken toys?

> > > > > > > > > > > > > > > > > > > >

Have the power to control the weather

OR

have the power to freeze time?

ONE FINAL THING...

Thank you for making it through to the end of
Would You Rather...? Book for Kids 6-12 Years Old, let's
hope it was fun, silly and able to provide you and
your family with all of the entertainment you needed
for this rainy day (or sunny afternoon)!

> >

Did you enjoy the book?

If you did, please let us know by leaving a review on
AMAZON. Reviews let Amazon know that we are creating
quality material for children. Even a few words and ratings
would go a long way. We would like to thank you
in advance for your time.

If you have any comments, or suggestions for improvement
for other books, we would love to hear
from you, and you can contact us at
riddleland@riddlelandforkids.com

Your comments are greatly valued, and the book has already
been revised and improved as a result of helpful suggestions
from readers.

Riddleland Bonus

Join our **Facebook Group** at **Riddleland for Kids**
to get daily jokes and riddles.

> > > > > > > > > > > > > > > > > > > >

https://pixelfy.me/riddlelandbonus

Thank you for buying this book. As a token of our appreciation,
we would like to offer a special bonus—a collection of
50 original jokes, riddles, and funny stories.

CONTEST

Would you like your jokes and riddles to be featured in our next book?

We are having a contest to discover the cleverest and funniest boys and girls in the world!

1) Creative and Challenging Riddles
2) Tickle Your Funny Bone Contest

Parents, please email us your child's "original" riddle or joke. He or she could win a Riddleland book and be featured in our next book.

Here are the rules:

1) We're looking for super challenging riddles and extra funny jokes.

2) Jokes and riddles MUST be 100% original—NOT something discovered on the Internet.

3) You can submit both a joke and a riddle because they are two separate contests.

4) Don't get help from your parents—UNLESS they're as funny as you are.

5) Winners will be announced via email or our Facebook group – **Riddleland for kids**

6) In your entry, please confirm which book you purchased.

Email us at **Riddleland@riddlelandforkids.com**

Other Fun Books by Riddleland
Riddles Series

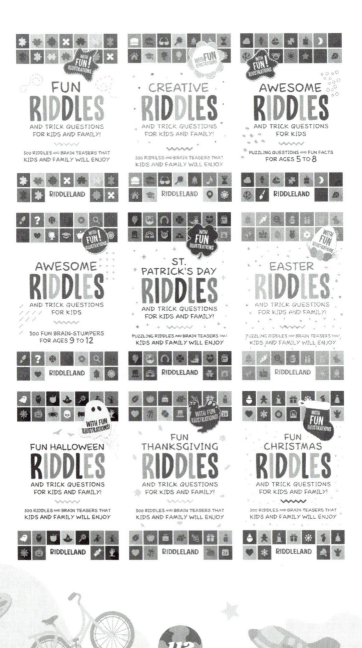

FUN **RIDDLES** AND TRICK QUESTIONS FOR KIDS AND FAMILY! 300 RIDDLES AND BRAIN TEASERS THAT KIDS AND FAMILY WILL ENJOY — RIDDLELAND

CREATIVE **RIDDLES** AND TRICK QUESTIONS FOR KIDS AND FAMILY! 300 RIDDLES AND BRAIN TEASERS THAT KIDS AND FAMILY WILL ENJOY — RIDDLELAND

AWESOME **RIDDLES** AND TRICK QUESTIONS FOR KIDS PUZZLING QUESTIONS AND FUN FACTS FOR AGES 5 TO 8 — RIDDLELAND

AWESOME **RIDDLES** AND TRICK QUESTIONS FOR KIDS 300 FUN BRAIN-STUMPERS FOR AGES 9 TO 12 — RIDDLELAND

ST. PATRICK'S DAY **RIDDLES** AND TRICK QUESTIONS FOR KIDS AND FAMILY! PUZZLING RIDDLES AND BRAIN TEASERS THAT KIDS AND FAMILY WILL ENJOY — RIDDLELAND

EASTER **RIDDLES** AND TRICK QUESTIONS FOR KIDS AND FAMILY! PUZZLING RIDDLES AND BRAIN TEASERS THAT KIDS AND FAMILY WILL ENJOY — RIDDLELAND

FUN HALLOWEEN **RIDDLES** AND TRICK QUESTIONS FOR KIDS AND FAMILY! 300 RIDDLES AND BRAIN TEASERS THAT KIDS AND FAMILY WILL ENJOY — RIDDLELAND

FUN THANKSGIVING **RIDDLES** AND TRICK QUESTIONS FOR KIDS AND FAMILY! 300 RIDDLES AND BRAIN TEASERS THAT KIDS AND FAMILY WILL ENJOY — RIDDLELAND

FUN CHRISTMAS **RIDDLES** AND TRICK QUESTIONS FOR KIDS AND FAMILY! 300 RIDDLES AND BRAIN TEASERS THAT KIDS AND FAMILY WILL ENJOY — RIDDLELAND

It's Laugh O'Clock Joke Books

Would You Rather...Series

Get them on Amazon or our website at
www.riddlelandforkids.com